THE DAY THAT CHANGED *My Life*

Helen Anderson

Published by Healing Rooms Scotland
PO Box 7010, Glasgow G76 0WF United Kingdom.
Telephone 0044 (0)141 637 4445
www.healingrooms-scotland.com

Printed in the United Kingdom
ISBN 978-0-9562397-3-0

Acknowledgements

Thanks to Jeanne and Andy Neal, who do a great job leading our Healing Rooms in East Kilbride, for their editing and suggestions.

Thanks to Diane West, who with her husband Andy lead two Healing Rooms in Fife, for her excellent grammar checks.

Thanks to our friends Alison and Andrew Gallacher for their proof reading.

Thanks to James Renwick for his excellent typesetting.

Thanks to our faithful supporters who have enabled us to step out into the new things God has led us into.

"I give thanks to God for Helen and endorse the testimony of what he has done in her life.

Thank you, Helen, for sharing your journey and the processing of your life story."

Jean Black, Director Pray for Scotland

THE DAY THAT CHANGED

My Life

Foreword

There are very few books which I will read cover to cover - literally "can't put it down" stuff - Helen Anderson's book is one of these. You are drawn in to this amazing story of desperation, devastation and depression but quickly sense that there is a very different end in sight.

Written by Helen in her own vibrant style, chapter by chapter I was left asking, "Then what happened?" What we find revealed in each page are the dynamic and transformative encounters of the living God with one of his beloved children. It truly is a story that will inspire hope and faith. If God can do this for Helen then what can he do for you?

Alongside this amazing storyline is the wisdom and insight that it has written directly on Helen's heart. Page after page is filled with powerful truths - learned through experience - of who God is and what he can do today. This book will encourage and inspire anyone who looks at their life and thinks, "Is this it?" Through her graphic storytelling Helen brings to life again and again the faithfulness, goodness and power of God.

This is a book which is full of hope, new possibilities and fresh purpose. I strongly encourage you to read this book and then pass it on to someone else. It really could change your life and theirs!

Alan McWilliam,
Chairman CLAN (New Wine Scotland)

- Chapter One -

He Knows My Name

THE door flew open and two ambulance men hurried into our home, restrained my Mum in a strait-jacket and proceeded to carry her off to the psychiatric hospital. As they were taking her from the living room, I, just a toddler, was cowering, curled up behind the sofa. I caught my Mum's eyes looking pleadingly at me as if silently calling out, "Help me, help me!" It was as if she was unable to speak with her mouth, but her helpless gaze pierced into my soul. I curled up even more tightly and thought to myself, "I can't help anybody." Deep inside, as I sobbed, feeling helpless and useless, I made a powerful and negative declaration over myself that I couldn't help anyone. This was one of my earliest memories. I don't

I made a powerful and negative declaration over myself that I couldn't help anyone

know how long my Mum was away that time, but this was to become the pattern of my childhood.

My mother had been diagnosed with severe post-natal depression after the birth of my older sister Sandie, but the treatments that she was given in hospital at this time seemed to have little or no effect. I was later told that the doctors had suggested to my father that having a second child would possibly cure his wife. I was that child and my birth did not cure my mother. In fact my mother's mental health continued to deteriorate and years later she was diagnosed with schizophrenia, spending much of her life in psychiatric hospitals.

My mother was full of fear and lived a very troubled life, having good spells when she was out working, but other times the darkness of depression would rule and ruin her life. Sometimes I'd come home from school and would know immediately if Mum was depressed or okay. If the house smelt of furniture polish and the radio was blasting out tunes, then everything would be good. However, if I walked into the room where my Mum was and she was sitting clicking her finger nails together and blankly staring into space, then I thought, "Oh no, it's here again," and fear would grip my heart.

I desperately wanted my Mum to be well, for things to be normal, at least how I thought normal might be, and to have some sort of meaningful communication with her. I longed to be asked how my day had been, how I was feeling and to feel safe and warm. The reality was that I barely remember having more than three meaningful conversations with my mother her whole life.

Although I was born in Glasgow, when I was still very young we moved to Johnstone a town about 15 miles south west of the city, where my father worked as a sheet metal worker and draughtsman along with my Grandfather, who was from Glasgow's East End. My father was a hardworking, clever man who had won prizes at school and in the Boys' Brigade. I always knew that my parents loved each other dearly and would never have thought that they would separate; a knowledge which brought a glow of security into my otherwise insecure heart. However, my Dad's life would soon take a huge downturn. We all have

How we respond to circumstances changes our lives, we can be victorious or we can be victims

choices. How we respond to circumstances changes our lives, we can be victorious or we can be victims. Sadly my father became a victim.

He started going to the local pub after work and having a few drinks before coming home. When he got his pay-packet on a Friday, he went to the local social club and began drinking more and more, until alcohol took a powerful hold over his life. By the time I was seven years of age he would often go on drinking binges spending much time with a group of local drinkers some of whom had no homes. They would frequently be in our house, drunk on cheap wine, creating total chaos and disruption for the whole family. One night in particular I remember lying in bed trying to sleep amid the din caused by several drunk men shouting and smashing bottles over each other. I took my pillow, grabbing each side and pulled it over my head and ears to try and drown out the noise. I called out to a God I wasn't even sure existed and prayed that he would shut them up. The next moment there was complete silence! For how long I don't know, but there was silence and my first ever prayer seemed to be answered.

During those early years, when my two younger brothers Archie and Andrew were born, family life seemed to consist of normal episodes interrupted by bouts of depression and binges of booze. It was like an emotional rollercoaster that left me feeling insecure, confused, and empty and lacking any stability.

I am not wholly sure what mix of factors caused my father to ruin himself with alcohol (which caused his untimely death at 57 years of age) or caused my mother's mental health condition. I have discovered that whatever the reasons were, I need to honour my mother and father and to forgive the failings I perceived in them. I am not entirely certain what were the actual circumstances surrounding my conception and birth, but I am certain, and now know deep in my heart that God, my Heavenly Father, had a great and awesome plan for my life, and that my birth was rejoiced over in heaven.

A section of the Bible has spoken very powerfully to me and become one of my favourite passages:

For you created my inmost being; you knit me together in my mother's womb.
I praise you because I am fearfully and wonderfully made; your works are wonderful,
I know that full well.
My frame was not hidden from you when I was made in the secret place,
when I was woven together in the depths of the earth.
Your eyes saw my unformed body; all the days ordained for

me were written in your book
before one of them came to be.
Psalm 139:13-16

So having been brought up in a dysfunctional home, being told my birth was supposed to have made my Mum better and declaring from a young age that I couldn't help anyone, I found the words of this psalm becoming a source of great healing to me. To read and to know, to understand and to believe that Almighty God, the Creator of the universe, had knitted me together, formed me, woven me and planned me was overwhelming.

This truth came to me powerfully, though at first painfully, one Christmas time. It was Christmas Day and I went with my husband Steven to visit my Mum in the hospital, leaving our two young children at Steven's parents' home. (Our third child had not been born at this time). When we went into my Mum's room she looked blankly at me and asked, "Who are you?" My Mum did not forget things, that wasn't part of her condition, but that morning for whatever reason she denied knowing my name. It pierced my heart like a sharp knife.

As we drove home I was distraught and sobbed and sobbed, while repeatedly saying, "She doesn't know my name, she doesn't know my name." However, later on I read these words of Psalm 139 and my Heavenly Father's love began to heal my heart.

A week or two later in early January, I was standing at the top of our stairs one Sunday morning when I heard a voice whisper in my ear saying, "You have a ministry to two year olds and under, to abandoned children." I wondered what this might mean, yet dismissed it fairly quickly from my mind. That evening we visited a small church near to us where Steven was speaking and a lady that I didn't know came up to me and said, "Hi, what's your name?" I answered, "Helen", and she told me that God had spoken to her that morning and said, "A girl is coming to the meeting tonight, her name is Helen, she has a pastor's heart and I know her name. Tell her that I know her name and that she has a heart for abandoned children".

I ran around everyone in that place, with a lit up face and bright eyes declaring loudly, "God knows my name, he knows my name"

I ran around everyone in that place, with a lit up face and bright eyes declaring loudly, "God knows my name, he knows my name." I felt like God zoomed into my life and healed me. There had seemed nothing more painful than that day when my own Mum didn't know my name, yet incredible healing and freedom came flooding into me when I truly knew that God knows me, knows my name and it was he who 'fearfully and wonderfully made me' in my mother's womb.

I may have had a largely negative perspective of the reason for my birth, a view that seemed to be reinforced by the insecurity of my early years, but I was to discover a whole new perspective as my eyes were opened to see from the Heavenly Father's vantage point. I came to understand that my birth was planned in God's design and purposed from heaven. The significance of my life still continues to unfold before my eyes as God works powerfully in me.

Whatever the circumstances of your birth, whether you were joyfully anticipated, wanted and loved or whether you were not wanted, considered 'a mistake,' or have experienced rejection, the truth is that there is a divine perspective that you need to come to see.

God is a Redeemer. Nothing and no-one need be lost. He can turn everything around and make it work for good. We see this happen in the lives of numerous people in the Bible, like Joseph who was sold into slavery and then imprisoned, before God redeemed the situation and Joseph got promoted to be in charge of all the affairs of Egypt. I thank God that he has redeemed my life and has worked, and continues to work, all things together for his good purposes.

When we come to Jesus he gives to us a new name and brings us into a new inheritance. No matter what name you were given, and no matter what 'names' have been spoken over you, God has a new name for you. When John the Baptist was to be born, his father Zechariah was told by an angel to call him John. There was no John in his family but God didn't want this mighty prophet to be limited by his ancestors. He was called John which means God is Merciful. Similarly an angel told Joseph that the child Mary carried in her womb was to be called Jesus, meaning the Lord Saves and Rescues, because *"he will save his people from their sins."* (Matthew 1:21). Whether you like your name or not is not the point here – the point is that God wants to name you, to give you identity and set the definition of who you are and what you can become in him.

No matter what name you were given, and no matter what 'names' have been spoken over you, God has a new name for you

God also has a new inheritance for you. In Jesus we become members of God's family and heirs of his Kingdom. Some people have received a great inheritance from their family line – that's wonderful, but God has even more for you! Others may have received little or even some harmful traits – the good news is that God has a whole new inheritance for you too. This inheritance is eternal life which is not just for us in heaven when we die but begins right now on earth as a new quality of life based on relationship with God as Father, with the resources of his Holy Spirit working in us. It is a life no longer based on fear, as mine was for so many years, but founded on faith and exploring and experiencing the favour of our loving Heavenly Father.

- Chapter Two -

Born to be a Princess

MY Grandfather would often say to me, "You were born to be a princess but dumped on the wrong doorstep." My sister Sandie and I were fostered by our grandparents and we spent a good number of years living with them in the East End of Glasgow. My life was far from settled. I went back and forth between my grandparents' house and my parents, attending different schools for periods of time.

When we were at my parents' home, we were in some ways just like an ordinary family; Mum, Dad, me, my sister Sandie and younger brothers Archie and Andrew living together in our three bedroom council house. At first Dad and Mum both worked, Dad alongside my Grandfather in a local factory and Mum as a machinist - which is kind of funny as I can hardly sew a button, far less work a sewing machine. (In fact in secondary school the home economics teacher was always shouting at me for breaking the machine needles). The family I desperately needed was one where there was the sense of belonging, security, safety, love and acceptance, a place where I could and should have been myself; a place where we would look out for one other and feel good in ourselves. Sadly, that wasn't the case for me and unfortunately isn't for lots of other people. There is no perfect family or perfect parent, but I have discovered a perfect Father and with his help I have found the healing, true security, love and acceptance I needed.

In those early days when Mum was ill, Sandie quickly stepped into the role of mother to me and my brothers. Many a time we would have arguments, as Sandie wanted me to help her clean the house but I just wanted to go out and play. I was about eight years old and she was only ten. These were the only times we disagreed as sisters. In those days I was really a bit of a tomboy. I would play 'kick the can' with the boys in the street and ride my bike without holding on to the handlebars. I had a wee daring streak in me and dreamed that, one day, I would be like an FBI agent! I actually did apply to work for Customs and Excise when I was eighteen and was offered the job, but then took a different one that paid more money. However, I was very lonely growing up with just one close friend, Rosemary, a Catholic girl who went to a different school. In the mornings I would walk with her to her school gate then on by myself to my own school.

After school each day as I went through the archway in our four in a block houses, and in by our back door, I would wonder what I was coming home to. Sneaking round I would listen to hear if there was the noise of drunken men. If there was, I'd sneak off again. Sometimes I'd just wander about the streets, other days I'd go to Rosemary's where it would be warm and I'd get fed. Our own home was at times without any electricity and heating and I became an expert at cooking potatoes and onions over a little gas camping stove. I remember other times when we had no electricity during the day, but my Dad ingeniously managed to wire our electric supply into the street lighting so when the street lights came, so did ours!

I recall one day, when I was in Primary 7, aged eleven years, my school teacher came to our door with homework. He was the first male teacher I'd had at school and to me he was the best. I loved the fact that he took an interest in everything about me. That day when he came to the house he stood at the door trying to look in and asked if everything was all right. (I now suspect he was checking on my home situation). I simply nodded yes, took my homework books and shut the door. Everything was not all right! My Dad was drunk, Mum was ill and I didn't know what to do.

Everything was not all right! My Dad was drunk, Mum was ill and I didn't know what to do

Many times the police were called by our neighbours and officers would arrive, coming in and going out at all sorts of times, even in the night. I was very fearful and would often go to bed holding my sister's long hair. We shared a bed together and I figured if someone came in to harm us I would feel my sister moving first. Outside in the street I portrayed a tomboy image, but inside I was a lonely and frightened little girl. I used to play a record in my room over and over again. The song went:

"I'm just a lonely boy, lonely and blue,
I'm all alone with nothing to do."

This seemed to sum me up – a lonely girl with no sense of security or meaning.

There was many a day when we would have no money in the house as my Dad, having now lost his job, relied on a social security cheque. As I appeared to be the boldest one in the family, outwardly at least, I would be sent round the neighbours to ask to borrow money until my Dad got his next cheque. This taught me a shamelessness and perseverance to ask, something which has become of great value in my life. Indeed I think this taught me what the Bible teaches, "You do not have because you do not ask." I have never lost that boldness to keep asking for what I need.

Our family situation deteriorated throughout my childhood and inevitably the social work department got involved. I remember one time being taken from our house and ending up in a young social worker's home. It was warm and I vividly recall the thick velvet curtains that hung in the living room. It seemed like a proper home, warm and safe. I determined then that my home would be like this when I grew up. I actually became a bit obsessed later in life when I became a mum myself, always making sure my children came home from school to a warm house, to a cup of milk and biscuits and I'd ask them what they'd done at school and what homework they had. I did all the things that I felt I had missed and would have wanted. I over-reacted so much at first that I'd drive my children nuts going on and on about homework and all the other things.

Eventually the family split up and, after a brief stay in a children's home, brief but long enough to leave an indelible and unpleasant impression on me, my two young brothers were fostered by a neighbouring family and Sandie and I were taken in by our grandparents.

I was living in the wrong place, not so much the house I was in, but in my own mind and thinking

My grandparents on Dad's side lived in one of the 'rough' areas of Glasgow's East End. Both of them worked. Instead of me going round the doors asking to borrow money, in that street it was to my gran's door that people came for a loan of money! My grandpa joked about me being a princess dumped at the wrong doorstep, which actually had a lot of truth in it. Indeed I am royalty, part of God's family and a daughter of the King of Kings. I was living in the wrong place, not so much the house I was in, but in my own mind and thinking. Although our grandparents loved us and looked after our physical needs, they weren't my Mum and Dad. I still wanted to be with my parents despite all their struggles and difficulties. I still desperately needed to have a sense of truly belonging.

As I entered my teenage years I began to mask some of the insecurity and fear. Outwardly, I would still display boldness and showed little fear. When a boy my older sister's age hit her, I ran down the street, jumped on his back and began hitting him! When my Dad was sleeping in a drunken stupor I would pour the cheap wine down the sink and empty the money out of his pockets in order to buy food. My life was not what I wanted it to be, but it was quite eventful at times! It all developed a strong tenacity and boldness in me, but alongside these qualities, my life was characterised by a deep rooted fear, instability, insecurity, loneliness and a deep longing to be someone else and to live somewhere else.

"My life was characterised by a deep rooted fear, instability, insecurity, loneliness and a deep longing to be someone else and to live somewhere else"

- Chapter Three -

Our Vulnerability: God's Victory

TWICE this longing to live somewhere else almost materialised. When I was 14 years old my aunt, my Dad's youngest sister, and her husband emigrated from Scotland to Australia and wanted to take me with them but my father wasn't keen on the idea and wouldn't let me go. Again, when I was 22 years old, I planned to go out to Australia and had been booked to go on the 1st of May, but changed my mind as the time approached. On the very day that I would have been flying across the world I met my future husband, Steven, in Glasgow. We met on the 1st of May; I think we fell in love on the 2nd of May. In less than ten months we would be married. I was entering a period of my life where things would change and at a rapid pace.

Growing up I had no knowledge of God or any understanding of the Christian faith. Gran went to the local Presbyterian Church and I would occasionally babysit for the minister and his wife, but that was it. Steven, on the other hand, had been brought up in a Christian home and taken to a local Baptist church where he had become a Christian and been baptised in his mid-teens. However, when we met he was quite far from God. It turned out God still had his hand firmly upon Steven! On some Sundays I began to go along to his church but didn't find it too exciting until one Sunday evening in the October of that year. It was a baptismal service where I think three people were being baptised by full immersion, that is going completely under the water and up again! My initial reaction was, "Forget that, you just get all wet."

I suddenly felt my heart beating faster and faster and something strange going on inside me

However, when the minister began to speak afterwards I suddenly felt my heart beating faster and faster and something strange going on inside me. Like John Wesley said, "I felt my heart strangely warmed." I really didn't have much of a clue about what the minister said; I simply knew I had to respond to God and give my life to Jesus. I found myself out of my seat and walking to the front of the church before I really knew what was going on. Chris, the minister, looked at me and asked my name. I felt so shy, and looking at my toes I muttered: "Helen." Chris said, "Pardon, I didn't catch that." Again I whispered, "Helen", and then he asked what I wanted to do. I said, "I want to give my life to Jesus." Chris told the people there what I'd said and two other people then responded, coming to faith in Jesus as well.

After the service a lady in the church took me aside to pray with me and I prayed my second ever prayer and asked Jesus to forgive my sin and come into my life. He did, and I felt a different person. A few weeks later I was baptised by full immersion, and yes, you do get very wet, but it was wonderful. I joined the church and in the following February (1982) Steven and I were married in that very church building. As I write this, we have just celebrated our 30th anniversary.

With these two new relationships, my life began to take on a new stability. I had a God who loved and gave himself for me, and a new husband who loved me and made me feel secure and special. I now had a new expectancy and a sense of adventure and purpose about my life. By the summer of 1982 big changes were afoot for us. We really wanted to start a family and I soon became pregnant with our first child, Michael. Around this time Steven was also feeling big shifts in his life. He was a sales representative for Cadbury's selling chocolate, but God was stirring his heart with a call to preach. This call was recognised by others and he started the process of applying to be trained to become a Baptist minister. That would mean him giving up his job at a time when I'd be leaving work soon to have a baby. However, I no longer felt insecure and was ready for the adventure of a lifetime. I was happy to go and live anywhere – I used to say, "We'll even live in a tent if we have to."

I now had a new expectancy and a sense of adventure and purpose about my life

As our baby grew within my womb, I looked forward so much to the day he would come forth into the world. I didn't officially know he was a boy, but I kind of knew anyway. I called him 'Wee Joe' at that time and I used to talk to him and tell him where we were and what we were doing. I was growing bigger and bigger and even went to a fancy dress party as humpty dumpty! 'Wee Joe' was the most wanted child I could imagine. I went into hospital in March 1983 to give birth to my own son full of expectation, anticipation and excitement.

Being a little overdue I was taken into hospital and induced and initially all seemed to be going to plan. However, 19 hours of labour later, the medical staff realised I was not going to give birth naturally as there was a problem which caused a blockage to the birth canal. Both our baby and I were in distress. I was rushed to theatre where a doctor performed a C-section and brought Michael into the world safe and sound. I was left totally exhausted.

My childhood friend, Rosemary, also had her first baby around that time. She was four weeks ahead of me and came with her new baby to visit me in the hospital. By this time, a few days after Michael was born, I was feeling helpless and unable to do anything. I remember thinking that Rosemary looked as if she coped so easily with her new baby and here was I feeling inadequate. Something seemed very wrong with me. People brought present after present and card after card, but I just wasn't interested and couldn't feel anything physically or emotionally. At first the hospital staff said it was baby

It became apparent I was suffering from deep depression

blues, but as the days went on it became apparent I was suffering from a deep depression.

After ten days in hospital I came home, but things were no different inside of me. When my Dad came to visit me I took him into the baby's room and said to him, "I think I'm going like Mum and I don't know how to cope." He looked blankly at me and walked back through to the living room. During my pregnancy I had kept saying to Steven, "Don't worry, I won't go like my Mum." Now I was not so sure about that.

Over the next few days nothing changed, I felt totally empty and as if there was no point to anything. Nothing seemed to make any sense. I'd go to bed but didn't sleep. I'd get up and each day would be the same. I thought I'd ruin Steven's life and it would be better if I wasn't here anymore. I was actually so depressed and unresponsive that Steven and his parents didn't know what to do. The midwife came to visit and check on me and the baby, as did a sister from the hospital who told me, "If you don't pull your socks up then you'll be going into Leverndale." - our local psychiatric hospital. Although this was a ridiculous thing for someone in her position to say, to me it was a relief. I just thought, "If I go into hospital then I'll be out the way and Steven can get on with his life." The doctor finally came and had me admitted to Leverndale hospital where I would spend the next four weeks.

It was the most terrifying experience of my life"

It wasn't a relief at all; in fact it was the most terrifying experience of my life. I would lie on my bed in a ward with the nurses talking at their station thinking the whole thing was imaginary. I thought it was a play and Steven had set all these characters up. I remember the first day in the hospital when the nurse ran a bath for me and asked if I liked it very warm or how I liked it. She gave me a strange look when I said, "I want it boiling hot." I actually thought these people were there to punish me and the boiling water would punish me with pain. I wouldn't eat and when Steven came to visit, I didn't say a word. A pastor's wife who we knew from a nearby church came and asked me if I knew who she was. I thought, "How silly, of course I know who you are." Although I said nothing to anyone, I knew exactly what everyone said to me and who visited and when, and what they were wearing. No-one got a word out of me; it was as if I had frozen inside.

While I was in hospital Steven was accepted to train at the Baptist College. Also my Gran, who had been ill for a while died, but I was unable even to attend the funeral. The day she died Steven came to visit me at the hospital, sat me on a bench in the grounds and told me he had something to tell me. I said to him first, "It's OK, I know, Gran's died hasn't she?" I never mentioned her death again for a long, long time.

The psychiatrist told Steven that he had never seen anyone so depressed and that I'd need to be in hospital for a year and on antidepressants for at least two years

During this time Steven met with the psychiatrist a couple of times and took me out for the day once or twice. The psychiatrist told Steven that he had never seen anyone so depressed and that I'd need to be in hospital for a year and on antidepressants for at least two years. However, Steven saw the fear and horror I was experiencing in the hospital and persuaded the doctor to let him take me home. He had handed in his notice to Cadbury's and left work in time for me coming home, so he could look after Michael and me.

It was good to be out of the hospital, but I was still very depressed and felt totally unable to cope with anything. Life was a blur. I felt I had been consigned to hell and still felt I was being punished. I was living in total darkness. I took the antidepressants for two days but they gave me a strange feeling in my head, so I stopped. (These days we would never suggest to anyone to just stop taking medication without consulting their doctor, but that is what I did). The truth was, I didn't need medication, I needed my wounded heart and soul healed. I needed healed from my fears, my insecurities and the judgements I had made towards Mum and myself.

Though I had become a Christian, I was not immune to depression. I had not been truly healed of my deep wounds and fears. God needed to go deeper in my life and truly transform me. The pain of my inner life had to be exposed so it could be cured. However, our vulnerability precedes God's victory.

Our vulnerability precedes God's victory

Over the months after being released from hospital, Steven did his best to care for me and Michael and his parents and their friends were praying fervently for me. Nothing seemed to be changing and it seemed that the words of the doctor were true, that I'd be like this for a long, long time. That was until one night in August 1983.

- Chapter Four -

When God Speaks

AT first it was like any other night. It was 2am and very dark. Like most nights at that time, I wasn't sleeping, and when Michael woke crying I went blindly through the motions of getting a bottle and began feeding him. I still felt lifeless, all seemed black and dark and I didn't feel any purpose to what I was doing. Suddenly I heard a voice that I knew I had heard before – the voice of God. He said one word: "Enough!" That was it, everything changed. The lights came on inside me, the depression vanished and I knew I was free. As the great hymn says, "My chains fell off, my heart was free, I rose went forth and followed thee."

He said one word: "Enough!"

This was the day, the moment that changed my life. I have followed Jesus wholeheartedly ever since and I have never experienced a day of depression since then. Steven had his wife back; I was alive!

This was the day, the moment that changed my life

A single word can have amazing power when it is spoken by the One with true authority. As our friend Allan McKinlay's song goes:

"When God speaks, mountains are moved, people are healed, hearts are set free."

The reality of what the Bible says came true in my life:

"He sent forth his word and healed them;
He rescued them from the grave."
Psalm 107:20

God is always sending forth his word to heal, to save and to set people free. We need to hear it, believe it and receive it.

I found life had now shifted from being stuck in a dungeon of dark depression, sitting at home, staring at the walls, to suddenly feeling free to face life, to go outside, to do the normal activities of shopping, walking and meeting and talking to people. Very soon afterwards we went for a few days holiday to Pitlochry in the heart of Scotland and called on the minister who had married us and baptised me. He had moved from our church in Glasgow a few months earlier, not long after Michael's birth, and he and his wife had come to see me a number of times at the outset of the period of depression. We called at his home unannounced and he answered the door with a paintbrush in his hand. He looked shocked both to see the three of us at his door and at the obvious transformation in me. Here I was - now a happy, secure and settled mother and wife enjoying a holiday in the beauty of Scotland's countryside.

Once we returned from this holiday Steven began his training at the Baptist College. This had seemed impossible for me just a few weeks previously, but now I had the confidence to be at home with Michael on my own, to care for him and even to be around other mothers without feeling that I was totally inadequate and useless. I continued to have visits from the health visitor and the hospital nurse who had previously told me to "pull my socks up." This nurse came into the house for the first time since that wonderful night and looked absolutely stunned as she fixed her eyes on me. Her mouth seemed to literally drop open. She said she had never seen such a change in anyone before, so much so that she told me about a service that provided support for mothers suffering post-natal depression, and asked if I would consider becoming a volunteer for this service. I did become a volunteer and this was just the start of God giving me a heart to see many people freed from the grip of depression and mental illness.

The depression was completely healed. God had brought the breakthrough, but there was still work for him to do. When God heals he wants to heal thoroughly, to the core, so that we can walk in long lasting freedom, health and fullness of life. He doesn't just deal with symptoms but gets to the root. There were roots in my life that needed his further healing and deliverance and along with this; he was preparing me for what lay ahead.

God had brought the breakthrough, but there was still work for him to do

Much happened in the next three to four years from 1984 to 1987. I gave birth to our second child, a beautiful daughter, Nicky. The consultant at the hospital brought Steven in and expressed his concerns about how I might be, fearing that the depression could occur again. I knew it wouldn't, I knew I was healed; I knew what God had done. There was not even a trace of depression this time. 1984 was a good year, it was a warm and sunny summer and we were living as a happy family.

The next two years however brought pain and grief into our lives, as first Steven's brother was killed in a mountaineering accident at the age of 27, then in the space of just ten months I lost my Grandfather, Dad and my young brother Archie who died at just 24 years of age. With my Grandfather's death and my Gran having died two years previously, the two most stable people in my upbringing were now both gone.

One day in February 1986, while Steven was at college, I'd planned to take our two small children to visit my Dad and Mum who were now living in my Grandparent's house in Glasgow's East End. My brother Archie was there with them at the time so I called ahead to check Dad was sober. As I was getting the children ready Archie phoned back and said, "Don't come, he's dead." I phoned Steven's Mum in a hysterical state, telling her that Archie had just told me that my Dad was dead and that they'd need to get right over and take care of the children. I phoned the Baptist College and asked for Steven. The secretary said that he was in a class and that I couldn't speak to him. I told her Dad was dead and, yes, I needed to speak to him right now. He came straight home and we went up to find the house full of police officers.

When we arrived we were taken aside by officers and quizzed about what might have happened, their whole tone being one of accusation and suspicion. They were trying to imply that Archie had been fighting with Dad and was somehow responsible for his death. We were all taken to the main police station where we were separated and made to feel like criminals. Mum, who was far from well, was questioned at length. She didn't really know what was going on and said she thought Dad had just broken his leg. Fortunately, during this ordeal one of the higher ranking officers, a friend of Steven's parents, came by where we were waiting. Things began to get sorted out and we were allowed home. At length the post mortem was carried out and the cause of death was clearly shown to be cirrhosis of the liver due to alcohol poisoning. Once this came through the suspicion was lifted but we were thoroughly shaken by the whole experience.

Archie continued to live in his own flat in Paisley near where we had grown up. My youngest brother Andrew was still with the foster family in Johnstone, though he and Archie were very close and saw a lot of each other. Later that year Steven and I were returning from a conference in England. When we stopped at a service station on the motorway Steven called his parents to check the children were alright. His Mum told him she had bad news, Archie had died. When Steven came back to the car he said nothing but I knew something was wrong. It was not until we got back to Glasgow and had called in at the house of a couple from the church that Steven told me the news. I burst into tears, pounded on his chest and cried out, "Who's next?" It seemed like every few months someone in my family was being wiped out.

Shortly before this painful and grief-filled season in my life, my sister Sandie had arranged a holiday for me and her along with both Archie and Andrew. It was the only holiday that I can actually remember spending together with my sister and brothers and turned out in the course of events to have been a very special time for us.

Being in relationship with Jesus doesn't hide us from or make us immune from life's struggles and pains. However, he does give us an amazing peace and strength through such times and events. Through all that happened during those years, my testimony has been that God was always there for me and that through the storms of this world, God is our refuge. Life may bring tragedy our way but God remains who he is - a good and loving Father - and proves himself to us when we open our hearts to his grace and truth.

God had other things to do in my life and more to teach me. He continued to bring healing to the depths of my soul and to show me how I could live this new life secure in his love. Our old ways and habits don't always go too easily and we can find ourselves reacting and falling into old patterns of thought and behaviour. Month by month the Lord worked the truth of his limitless love into the very fabric of my soul. He confronted my fears and delivered me from them. He wants to transform lives from having a fear-based foundation to being founded on the basis of the height, depth, length and breadth of his love.

Month by month the Lord worked the truth of his limitless love into the very fabric of my soul

Through the years that Steven was training for ministry we were to begin to learn about God's provision for us as a family. Before Michael was born we were both working – Steven was a sales representative and I was an international operator for British Telecom. In a very short space of time we went from two salaries to having only a small student grant. I had often known lack and poverty as a child and I didn't want my children to experience that. I remember one day when we had no money and no food in the house. Our family allowance was due the following Monday and I prayed that God would give us just £10 to buy food over the weekend so my children wouldn't go through what I did at times. No-one but God heard that prayer, yet within an hour or so, a small unmarked envelope came through our letterbox. Inside was only one thing – a brand new £10 note! Over the coming months and years God would show himself to be incredibly faithful in supplying our needs. Every time that God teaches us these lessons he is preparing us for something more, for the next stage.

Every time that God teaches us these lessons he is preparing us for something more, for the next stage

I wasn't alive to please people but to please the One who took true pleasure in me

God also had to prepare me for what would be thrust upon us in 1987 when Steven became the minister of the Baptist Church in Castlemilk. Money is easy for God to deal with, but people can be quite different! Becoming 'the pastor's wife' brought a new pressure into my life. Was this really me? What did people expect of me? A lot of the old insecure feelings wanted to arise again. At times it was a steep learning curve, but the Lord taught me well. Not so much about what to do and to say, but about who I really was in him. I was born to be a princess, I was his daughter, his treasured possession and I belonged to him. I wasn't alive to please people but to please the One who took true pleasure in me. The verses of 1 Peter 2:9 became very precious to me:

But you are a chosen people, a royal priesthood, a holy nation, a people belonging to God, that you may declare the praises of him who called you out of darkness into his wonderful light.

- Chapter Five -

It's Time to Fly

GOD was opening up a whole new world to me, one filled with possibilities and opportunities. I had a growing understanding of my true identity in Jesus, a new realisation of the significance and purpose that my life could have, and a growing understanding that I could now bring healing and freedom to others. I was discovering the joy of partnering with God's Holy Spirit to heal the sick, to speak words of life to others and was finding myself in some surprising places. God wants to stretch and expand every one of us.

God wants to stretch and expand every one of us

In 1989 I visited Kenya, along with Steven, speaking in various churches. It was quite a change from what I'd been used to. Our church usually had about 30 people there on a Sunday but here I would stand up in front of congregations of 3,000. The climate was of course very different too – the sun shone all day! One day I managed to let myself get dehydrated and collapsed banging my head on a concrete floor, where I lay unconscious for a few moments. I discovered on a trip to a hospital in Glasgow a few years later that there was an old hairline fracture in my skull, presumably caused by this event!

A couple of years later we travelled to the south of England to attend a conference in Brighton. The last time I'd been to a conference in England I came back to the news of my brother's death. This time as we travelled back I could hear, with the sound of the train, a voice that seemed to come from within me saying over and over, "Bless the fruit of your womb, bless the fruit of your womb." Our two children, Michael and Nicky were now eight and seven years old and we had not planned to have any more children, but God appeared to have other ideas and a year or so later our lovely daughter Suzie was born. Again there were no problems and absolutely no depression.

Around this time, a team of folks from our church took over a Sunday night soup run in the centre of Glasgow. We would take hot home-made pies, hot drinks and chocolate biscuits to those sleeping rough in the city and to the girls working on the streets. It was often late at night on the dark streets of the city that we witnessed God do miraculous things. We saw the power of heroin addiction broken and legs swollen through injecting drugs immediately decrease to normal. One girl who was about to go into hospital to have a leg amputated was totally healed. We saw her some years later – she still had two legs, was now off drugs and was working as a drug counsellor.

It was often late at night on the dark streets of the city that we witnessed God do miraculous things

We were seeing God do miracles in the course of the work of our church. In our living room, Steven and I would see depression healed, numerous people set free from demonic spirits, physical healings and many set free from the inner wounds that were dominating and ruining their lives. We even went regularly into the psychiatric hospital where I had been those years before and would speak with many people about God's love and forgiveness and pray with them. It was such an amazing turnaround for me to walk through the doors of a place that had filled me with such terror and pain, but now to be coming in as a representative of the true Healer and Life-Giver, Jesus Christ.

God is always preparing us for more, for the extension of his Kingdom on earth.

God is always preparing us for more, for the extension of his Kingdom on earth

A few years later, God led us to begin Healing Rooms in Scotland, training up teams all over the nation and releasing his healing as a sign of the Kingdom throughout the land. In this work we have seen personally, and know of, so many healings and lives being transformed. We have seen cancer healed, arthritic pain vanish, damaged livers restored, short legs being lengthened, curved spines straightened, deaf ears hearing again and much more. Not everyone we pray with is healed, but many are, as God is leading us forward in the extension of his Kingdom. Jesus is the Healer who works through those who believe and the standard that he set is what we aim towards. In the Gospel of Matthew it says:

Great crowds came to him, bringing the lame, the blind, the crippled, the mute and many others, and laid them at his feet; and he healed them.
Matthew 15:30

Jesus is still healing today and nothing is impossible for him. No-one and no condition are beyond his reach. (Steven's book *Releasing Healing* gives much more teaching and testimony of God's healing power.)

Jesus is still healing today and nothing is impossible for him

God sends forth his word to heal, to transform and to bring life, so it's really important that we are listening to him. Over the years God began to train my ears to hear his voice more and more. I knew the power of his word spoken into my spirit, but also knew he wanted to release the power of his word to others through me. I was at a meeting one day where a woman who moved in the gift of prophecy was speaking. She picked me out and began to speak into my life. She said, "You're a mouth and your mouth has gotten you into a lot of trouble." That was very true! I had often opened my mouth when I should have kept quiet, and yes, it had got me into trouble at times. This lady went on to say, "You've tried to keep your top lip and bottom lip together and you've been caged up. Now it's time to fly and God will use you to speak."

A while after this I went to a gathering for church leaders near Glasgow where the speaker was a man called Jim Paul, from the Toronto church that had seen a great move of God's Spirit. After he spoke he got us all to stand and wait on the Lord. He came over to me and whispered in my ear, "You have a word for the women of Scotland, speak it." He held the microphone in front of my mouth and waited for an age. I stood there thinking, "Sorry, but you've got the wrong person." After a long silence I felt something in my stomach rise up and I spoke out words in a way I'd never done before. That was the start of something. I often sense that same feeling in my stomach, and I now know it is the Spirit of God releasing his words of prophecy through me.

"Now it's time to fly and God will use you to speak"

By this time our church was experiencing a move of the Holy Spirit, which was particularly evident at our prayer meetings. The power of God would often fall on people and he would lead us in prayer for many different things and situations. He also spoke regularly to me in the shower! God 'speaks' in various ways and at all sorts of times and all kinds of places.

On the morning of New Year's Day in 1995 I saw, in a vision, a woman who looked as if she were from another country. Her eyes were pleading for help and she was saying, "Come over and help us." I heard God's voice say that this was for Albania. Geography has never been my strong point and I had no idea where Albania was, but something in my spirit told me that I could and would make a difference. All those years ago I saw my mother's eyes pleading with me to help and I couldn't. Now again I was seeing pleading eyes, but this time with God's strength I could do something to help.

In the April of that year I was at a prayer meeting in Glasgow led by a couple who became great friends and mentors to us, David and Jean Black. David announced that Jean and a small team were going to Albania to pray round the nation. I felt an excitement stir within me, but knew it wasn't time for me to go right then. However, over the next two years in our church prayer meetings we would often pray for Albania. I kept going on and on about Albania and we planned to go there and connect with one of Jean Black's contacts. I would not give those around me any rest till my feet touched the soil of Albania and, in 1997, I planned to head out along with two others from our church. We were still wondering what Albania might look like, when suddenly scenes of civil unrest in that land burst onto our television screens.

The unrest meant it wasn't safe for us to go there at that time but I'd been given another vision, this time a picture of Ann, the wife of the previous pastor of our church, waving us off on the journey. She and her husband David were now in south east Italy near to a port from which you could sail to Albania. We had felt it was God's direction to follow that route but the unrest meant we actually went to South East Italy where we discovered thousands of Albanian refugees in camps. We took the money we had been given, bought tons of towels and nappies from the local markets, and took them to the mothers and children in their need.

The following year I finally made it to Albania, this time with my friend Myra, who had been on the previous trip to Italy and another couple from our church. Just before going, while at a meeting with some church leaders, they prayed for me and one man said, "When you get there you will meet a 'man of peace'." We arrived at Tirana airport where we were met by a pastor with whom we'd been connected by someone else in Scotland. We met with several leaders and ministries over the time but our main contact was with Pellumb in a city called Elbasan - which is was a two hour drive over the mountains from Tirana. We weren't too sure how we'd get there.

We were staying with a church leader and the night before we were due to travel a young man arrived at the door. He had felt he should travel from Elbasan to Tirana to see this pastor, whom he knew, but he wasn't really sure why. It turned out he had come for us! He escorted us on the bus the next day and made sure we got safely to Elbasan. There we met Pellumb who introduced himself saying, "My name means 'dove, peace'." We stayed with this 'man of peace' and ministered in his church. One night we thought we were wakened by thunder though it sounded like gunfire. In the morning Pellumb assured us it was gunfire, a regular occurrence there at the time.

Back home God continued to lead us on the adventure that comes from following his voice and simply co-operating with what he is doing. We would, on occasions, climb the hill opposite our little church building to pray over the estate. One day I was up there praying with Steven and one of the church elders, Duncan. I suddenly 'saw' light bulbs go on in some of the houses in one particular street. I turned excitedly to Steven and Duncan and asked if they could see these lights too. They looked fairly blankly at me and said they could see nothing. However, we believed that God was turning on some lights in people's lives and we prayed for the families living in those particular houses. Over the next few weeks we saw people from each of those homes come to the church and come to faith in Jesus Christ.

One of those was Gail whose twins were in the same nursery school class as our youngest daughter, Suzie. Suzie and the twins became good friends and I got to know Gail. She lived in one of the 'light bulb' houses and I shared what God had shown me. One day when I was visiting her I asked to use the bathroom. She told me to be careful because the light wasn't working, but when I went in and pulled the cord the light came on! Very soon after she became a Christian, was baptised and then became the manager of our church café.

Another time when Steven and I were up the hill praying, I said to him, "Lift up your eyes, there's a whole city out there." Steven had been very focused on our local area of Castlemilk but God was calling us further out. Over the next while we began to initiate more prayer for our city, gathering church leaders to pray together. God began to show us things for the city and one night I had a dream about a spiritual battle taking place over George Square, the very centre point of Glasgow. In the dream God's victory came through extravagant praise and extreme generosity. These have continued to be a major focus for us. As we give praise to God and give away, so we position ourselves to receive the 'more' that God has for us.

As we give praise to God and give away, so we position ourselves to receive the 'more' that God has for us

This prayer ministry began to become our main focus and in 1999 we realised that God was calling us to leave our church and give ourselves fully to this new venture, which we called 'Prayer for the City'. God told me we were to step out of the boat and that we wouldn't drown, not an easy thought for me, a non-swimmer at the time. We knew we had to leave the church, the salary and the security of the church house where our family lived. We didn't know where we'd live or how we'd get any income but the Lord told Steven that he wasn't to ask anyone for any money or support; God would supply all our needs. So, we rented a house a few miles away and off we went on the next stage of the adventure.

- Chapter Six -

More than Enough

I was in the kitchen filling up the washing machine and as I put the scoop into the soap powder box I heard the voice of God say to me, "Like the widow's oil, my provision for you will never run out." (The story of Elijah and the widow can be found in 1 Kings 17:7-24). This was shortly before we left the church-owned house and moved to our first rented accommodation. When we moved into the rented house I went out to the shed in the garden and inside found, unopened, the largest box of soap powder I had ever seen – it was huge! I called the landlady, told her she had left this behind and asked if she wanted to come and collect it. She didn't seem to know anything about it and told me just to use it myself. We lived in that house for six months and, needless to say, never had to buy any soap powder!

It was now a new millennium, a new season for us and we were moving to new places. We had three children still at school and no regular income. At one time we did enquire at our bank if we might get a mortgage to buy a house. The bank manager found our faith, optimism as she saw it, quite amusing and suggested we come back in a couple of years once we knew what our income would be!

Just before we left the church, I had been working in a part-time job with the Community Mental Health branch of the Social Work Department. I worked up to fifteen hours a week and, once Steven resigned as Pastor of the church, this was our only income. I loved the work and the people with whom I came in contact. Those I visited were suffering from various types of mental health problems and most had very low self-esteem. They had no confidence to go out on their own so I would take them to places they needed to go - like the dentist or doctor, or sometimes to the cinema or the shops. I had the delight of going with one lady to choose the outfit for her son's wedding. What a joy it was to see her lift her head, look in the mirror and say, "I look nice. My son will be proud of me." Little by little I saw some of those 'captives' coming into a new freedom.

Little by little I saw some of those 'captives' coming into a new freedom

Another lady I met would never go out and used a wheelchair to get around the house. We had arranged for our Albanian friend Pellumb and his wife, Lindita, to come over to visit us in Scotland. I took them to visit this lady and she let Pellumb pray for her. After prayer she was able to get out the wheelchair, began to walk around the house and even started going out again. Another lady, whom I took to the church's café, asked me if she could just live there as she felt such a peace when she went into the building. I was very happy doing this little job and used to tell my boss stories of what God was doing in my life. However God had other plans for me and I'd soon have another story to tell my boss.

One Sunday evening Steven and I went to a church preaching engagement twenty miles away. Steven spoke about a man called Epaphras in the Bible, who worked diligently for the Lord and was always wrestling in prayer (Colossians 4:12-13). I prayed a silent prayer and said, "Lord, I want to do that, but I have to juggle the family, the ministry and my job." Then I prayed and said, "Lord, if I get a cheque for £500 I'll know I've to quit my job and go full time with Steven in the ministry".

Later that evening when we got home Steven's parents were at our house with the family. They told me that a gentleman had called by earlier and left an envelope for us. I opened the envelope which contained a short note saying that this gift was to help us in this time of transition. Inside was a cheque for £500! I let out a scream and dropped the cheque on the floor. The next day I went to my boss, told her the story and resigned from the job. Later I called the man who had sent the cheque to thank him and he told me he had been meaning to bring it for three weeks but he'd been unwell and that was the first day he could get out of the house.

It was a time of transition in so many ways. We had been almost thirteen years in the church house, but now we were in rented accommodation, doing a new ministry and wondering how everything would work out. One evening we went to one of the churches in Glasgow that was very supportive of our new prayer work in the city. A prophetic minister was there that night and the pastor, who knew us well, suggested that this man pray for us afterwards. As he did, he prophesied over us that he saw many boxes being packed as if we were moving. He also said he saw lots of sheep – both in the natural and the spiritual sense. We thought, "We've just moved so what's he talking about?"

We went on holiday soon after that and while away, we both had the sense that we wouldn't be going back to the house we were in. Our daughter, Nicky, was working with horses at a farm a few miles up the road. On the farm was a cottage, and when I picked her up one day I joked, "Maybe the cottage will become vacant and we could just move up here." No sooner had I returned home than the lady from the farm called me. She said that the man who rented the cottage was now leaving and asked if we'd be interested in renting it. It seemed very much the right thing to do. So after just six months the boxes did get packed again and we moved up among the horses and lots of sheep! From the windows of the house, which was situated on the moorland well above Glasgow, we could see almost the whole city, except the West End - where Glasgow University is located.

I was out shopping one day when in a shop window I saw a lovely framed print of the whole area around the University and the West End of the city. It cost £50 so I said to Steven, "If we get £50 unexpectantly, then I'm going to buy that so I can then see the whole city in and from my living room." Three days later we were speaking at another church and at the end of the evening a lady came up to me, shook my hand and said that she wanted to bless me. When she moved away I looked in my hand and there was £50!

As a little girl I had asked for money round the neighbours, now I was asking for the transformation of a city

I began to pray fervently over our city from our high place on the farm. One day in a vision two angels picked me up and flew with me over the city. They said to me, "This is your city, but you are to ask for it." All through my life God has been teaching the simple truth that we just need to ask him and we will receive. As a little girl I had asked for money round the neighbours, now I was asking for the transformation of a city.

God used that cottage to give me a perspective of the land as I prayed, but again it was to be a relatively short time before we were packing boxes again for our third move in less than two years. We were becoming experts at packing and moving. Again we moved because of revelation that God brought to me. It was Mother's Day and in the early hours of the morning I had a dream. I saw Steven's parents' home with workmen going in and out and an extension being built onto the back of the house. I saw

Steven's father in the dream who said to me, "This is the father's house and it's a safe place to be."

That morning we went to church and the preacher spoke from Luke chapter two about Jesus being in the Father's house. Then Steven's parents came up to the farm for lunch and I had a chat with his Dad. He told me that he had been going up the stairs the other day and thought to himself, "Why are the two of us in this house with more than enough space when the family is up the road paying out rent?" So the extension got built and we moved in together in 2001. I am glad to say that was the end of the moves and we could settle, at least in terms of a home.

Over the course of many years, we had witnessed God's provision and he was clearly training us to rely fully on him. Years before, when we lived in the church's house, we needed extra space so that Steven could have a study. His Dad came up with the idea of building a room inside the garage and priced the materials at £400. That was a lot back then - far more than we could afford. I told Steven to ask his Heavenly Father for what he needed. He prayed that Saturday night for the money needed for the study to be built. The following day a couple in the church asked to come and see us. They came down to the house in the evening and the wife sat fidgeting with her handbag. She then took out an envelope, handed it to Steven and told him she'd been putting money aside and last night she felt God told her to come and give it to him for whatever he needed it. Inside the envelope was exactly £400!

Whether it is relatively small amounts of money or very large, the same God cares and can provide when we ask; trusting, believing and relying on him. Another time in the church we were expanding the outreach work and developing a café and drop-in centre in the building. We really needed someone to come to develop and run this with us. We were praying about the provision for a salary for such a worker when someone in the church came to us and said she believed God had spoken to her saying, "Tell Steven that when he sees the crocuses bud and bloom, he will see the hand of God's provision." This was January and over the next few weeks we watched for the crocuses popping up and beginning to bud. It was then someone came with part of an inheritance they had received and gave £32 000 for us to bring in a new worker.

As we stepped out of the boat we were not going to drown.

As we stepped out of the boat we were not going to drown

Several people called over the first months of the new ministry and started to give monthly support. What we received from this and a few other irregular gifts was always just enough each month. If we had an extra expense then an extra gift always came. One day our car needed a new exhaust which cost £99. As we went to collect and pay for the car, not having a spare £99, we called by the post office box to collect our ministry mail. We opened a letter which was from a couple we barely knew and inside was a cheque for £100 – enough and a pound to spare!

God is our Shepherd and our Provider. He looks after us very well and is always preparing us for increase. Over the years we have had a small number of wonderful and faithful supporters whom God has prompted and led to give to us. When a supporter has stopped we have always seen someone else come forward to support us almost immediately.

One day, as I was vacuuming the stairs, I sensed God wanting to talk to me. I stopped and listened as he told me that one of our key supporters was about to stop giving to us, but that I should not worry as he was in this. The following Monday we went to have supper with friends who were supporting us at the time. They both seemed unusually nervous and one said to the other, "Will you tell them?" Eventually the wife blurted out that they were really sorry, but they weren't able to give to us any longer.

I sat on their couch and laughed and laughed. They thought it was a nervous laugh until I told them what the Lord had said to me the other day. Two days later I got a call from another person to say that she and her husband wanted to support us each month and that they'd send the first month's gift by cheque. A cheque duly arrived for twice as much as the support that had just stopped.

God can and does supply our every need, yet there is more. He loves generosity and he gives generously to us, releasing us to bless and to give to others. He is the God of more than enough. I love that word 'enough.' It was the powerful word God spoke over me as he freed me from the chains of depression. Our testimony is that God's supply has always been enough for every payment needed. Now he was going to show me more.

He is the God of more than enough

It was spring of 2007. On the Sunday morning when the clocks go forward an hour for British Summer Time, I awoke very early, my eyes sprung open and I was suddenly very wide awake and alert. I sensed a voice say to me, "Get up and give thanks to God for he is good and his love endures forever." At first I was reluctant, as everyone else in the house was fast asleep and I didn't want to disturb them.

But I felt my eyes had been enlarged to see something so I got out of bed and made my way downstairs.

As I entered our living room I had a phenomenal experience. It was as if I suddenly birthed butterflies from my stomach. I heard this whooshing noise from my stomach and I could see in a vision hundreds of butterflies flying around the room. Each one was beautiful and they had large, strong wings. They seemed sturdy and the different colours flowing through each one were amazing. I sat down on the couch and declared, "Lord, you are good and your love endures forever."

Then our living room appeared to be full of every flower you could imagine. The flowers were in full bloom and the colours were spectacular. Our living room had become the most beautiful garden. This vision is as clear to me today as it was then. Again I said, "Lord you are good and your love endures forever." Then God spoke to me and said, "Yes Helen, you have seen my faithfulness and you have paid every bill, but today I say to you 'I am the God of more than enough.'."

God wants to move us ever forward, advancing in the life of his Kingdom.

God wants to move us ever forward, advancing in the life of his Kingdom

Jesus came to give life, but not just life where we barely survive. He came to give life in all its fullness (John 10:10). He wants every one of us to know and live out this true life, this life of abundance where we are connected to, and in relationship with, the very source and author of life. He supplies our needs so we can live in freedom and focus on living out the wonderful purpose that he created for each one of us.

- Chapter Seven -

A Heavenly Encounter

LATER in 2007, I sensed that God wanted to communicate something more to me that was very important - but I needed to get away in order to listen to him. God does lead us and speak to us through the Bible, but the Bible itself says that we will prophesy and have dreams and visions (Acts 2:17-18). God can speak to us anywhere and in various ways. Initially I thought I should go away to some remote, quiet place to hear God's voice, but I ended up travelling with a whole bunch of folks to a conference with hundreds of other people.

God can speak to us anywhere and in various ways

Friends in Ireland had booked to go to a conference in Toronto at the end of October and Steven suggested I should link up with them for the journey. I mentioned this to a few friends back home and before long there were seventeen of us booked up. It was a good conference with great worship times and anointed speakers, but I was really there to hear from God, and that would happen in less than one hour during the second day of the conference.

At one of the meetings, John Arnott, who was leading the conference, called for all the pastors to come out to the front. I wasn't going to go up but one of my friends nudged me and said, "You are more of a pastor and leader now than you have ever been," so I went to the front along with many others. When John Arnott laid his hands on me I felt the power of God's Spirit rest on me and I fell backwards and lay there on the carpet. What happened next was not what I expected, but was to make a profound impact on my life.

I became quite oblivious to my surroundings and instead of hearing the worship group playing, I could now hear angels singing. I sensed they weren't with us in the conference room, but were in heaven. The next moment it was as if I was on the shores of the Sea of Galilee alongside Jesus and great crowds of people. He began to perform his miracles and I felt I was witnessing them first hand.

The next moment it was as if I was on the shores of the Sea of Galilee alongside Jesus

First it was the story of the loaves and fishes and I saw Jesus taking the bread, breaking it and multiplying it to feed the multitude. Then Jairus came along beseeching Jesus to come and heal his dying daughter. Jesus looked deeply into his eyes and said, "Don't be afraid, only believe." I could feel the strength and the impact of his words. Then a woman came and touched the edge of his cloak and I knew it was the woman with the issue of blood. (If you are not familiar with these Bible stories then see Mark 5:21-43.) I could actually feel the power and strength flow out of Jesus, going into the sick woman as he healed her. It was as if I were there. It all felt so very real, not like watching the Jesus movie but actually being present with him.

Then the vision switched and I saw a throne. On the throne was a lamb, pure and white, yet with blood flowing from his side – the Sacrificial Lamb. As I gazed upon him I wanted to weep, a deep heart felt weeping, but someone touched my shoulder and said to me, "Do not weep, behold the Lion of the tribe of Judah has triumphed." (see Revelation 5:5). Then I saw the Lion. His face seemed massive and his mouth was wide open as if he were about to roar, his long mane flowed down either side of his face.

Then my eyes were drawn to the left and I saw clouds parting and a staircase coming down, it was wide and steep and was as white as white could be. Jesus was at the top of the staircase and I could see his eyes which were blazing with pure fire. As he started to come down the stairs, my whole body shook and shuddered. I had been aware that I had been lying perfectly still, but now I was shaking and my arms and legs jerked. I felt that I was about to die. I spoke out and said, "Lord, have you come to take me? Am I about to die?" He replied, "No, I want to show you things." He took me by the hand and we went up three stairs, then he lifted me by my waist and put me at the top of the staircase. He was so big and I seemed so small.

At the top he took me by the hand and we began to walk together. I looked up at him and said, "Lord, I'm thirsty." He said, "That is not a problem as I am the fountain of life." Then a huge fountain of what seemed to be thick, bubbling, gurgling water appeared right before me and I walked through it with my mouth wide open. I drank and drank and was completely saturated and refreshed on the inside, yet was completely dry on the outside. Then I said, "Lord, I'm hungry." He told me not to worry, for he was the Bread of Life. An enormous brown loaf appeared before me and I ate and ate till I was totally full and satisfied.

We moved on together and came to a garden. It seemed to be the beautiful garden of my previous vision with all the flowers and butterflies, but now there were even more colourful butterflies. I just wanted to stay there as I loved it so much, but Jesus said, "No, come, there's more. There's always more." We went along roads with houses that had their doors flung wide open and many rooms inside. I wanted to go in and see what was there but again he told me, "No." and called me to come and see more that he had to show me.

Jesus said, "No come, there's more. There's always more"

Finally he took me to a throne where the kindest, softest, Gentle Man was sitting and Jesus brought me to him and sat me on his lap. This Gentle Man wrapped his arms lovingly around me and he and Jesus smiled at each other. Then he said, "Now we can release you, now you know what to do." As he said this, four angels appeared carrying a four poster feather bed and he laid me on it, at which point I came out of the vision, suddenly aware once more of my surroundings. Much had gone on while I was caught up in the Spirit. About forty minutes had passed though it seemed only a few moments to me. (Paramedics had been in and out of the building to attend to someone, yet I had been totally unaware of any commotion).

Now some people might wonder what this 'experience' was all about and whether it was for real or just my fertile imagination. I don't know whether this was a vision, some sort of heavenly encounter or what it should be called, but I do know what I saw and felt and the impact it had on me. Afterwards I felt full to overflowing and could hardly eat. I was bursting at the seams with excitement, joy and life. Parts of the Bible had come to life for me more than ever before and will live in my mind for the rest of my life. The God of the Bible doesn't want us just to read about him, but to know, encounter and experience him; to be the One who impacts every part of our lives.

God doesn't want us just to read about him, but to know, encounter and experience him

What was God was showing me in this vision? Why those three specific miracles and not some of the many others that Jesus performed? I see these miracles and these people's encounters with Jesus as highlighting his provision, peace and power. The feeding of the 5 000 showed me his miraculous provision, which is something that I have experienced and spoken of a lot in this book.

The words of Jesus to Jairus, whose twelve year old daughter had just died, are still very powerful for me today. Jesus did not speak empty words as he raised the girl back to life. It was those words, "Don't be afraid, only believe," that were so emphasised and penetrated so deeply. He is speaking these words all the time. He wants to address our fears and call us to faith. These are some of the most important words for his people to hear in this time. Sometimes we reach a place of desperation like Jairus, feeling overwhelmed or out of our depth, or life's events are out with our control. It's then that Jesus wants to meet us and speak these words of comfort, invitation and challenge into our hearts.

He wants to address our fears and call us to faith

The third miracle, of the healing of the woman who had been haemorrhaging for twelve years, highlighted for me the power that flows from Jesus. As she simply touched the edge of his cloak, power flowed into her and she was instantly healed. She didn't have to go through any rigmarole, but simply stretched out her hand in faith. Jesus' healing power is freely available today for those who believe with a childlike simple faith.

Jesus' healing power is freely available today for those who believe with a childlike simple faith

In Revelation chapter 5, Jesus is presented as the Lamb and the Lion. Side by side, these images are incredibly powerful. He is the triumphant, victorious, overcoming Lion of Judah, but his victory comes not through the brute strength we often associate with a lion, but through sacrifice, suffering and death. He is the Lamb of God who takes away the sin of the world. The Sacrificial Lamb is truly powerful. Here is the wonder of the Cross and the glory of the Resurrection.

What does the staircase represent? Like Jacob's ladder (Genesis 28:10-17), this represents a flow of revelation from heaven to earth. God comes down to speak and shows us things – if we are listening and looking. Like John the Apostle, he calls us up in the Spirit to share his perspective and his insights (see Revelation 4:1-2).

I felt both thirsty and hungry in the vision. Though this was a physical hunger and thirst, we all thirst and hunger to know God truly and have him satisfy the deepest longings of our souls. Many people seek to fill this longing with various comforts and distractions, but nevertheless it is still there. Jesus provides us with living water not in a cup that runs out, but in an everlasting fountain (see John 4:7-14). He is the eternal source. He is also the Bread of Life (see John 6:35) who feeds and nourishes our whole being. People feed themselves with all manner of things; feeding their minds and souls with much that pollutes, like feeding their bodies on a diet of junk food. Jesus provides true nourishment for our life, as we feed on him and his words.

Jesus provides us with living water not in a cup that runs out, but in an everlasting fountain

I briefly stopped in the beautiful garden and I would have stayed there, but Jesus called me on. This was the garden I recognised previously which was familiar and beautiful to me. We have a tendency to stop short, to remain where we feel good and secure, and by so doing, we can miss much more that God has for us. Jesus continually drew me forward, there was more that he wanted to show me.

The throne told me of God's rule. It showed he is in control and is not threatened by anything or anyone. It is of course a throne of glory but also a throne of grace. He rules not with an iron fist, but with everlasting arms of love, the arms I felt wrap around me. The feather bed was especially meaningful to me. It seemed to be the climax of the vision and highlighted a place of rest. I have often been busy, driven along by the many demands of life and ministry. But God wants me first and foremost to rest in him and to be still in his presence, waiting to hear his voice and to be led by his Spirit. It is not our busyness that will produce fruit, but our response to the Lord's initiatives. God desires our simple obedience to his voice, not our frantic activity.

Finally the Lord released me, saying that now I knew what to do. He wants to release us, giving us permission and a commission to make a difference in our world. Do I know what to do now? In one sense, no, I don't instinctively know what to do in any given situation, but in another sense, yes, I know to rest in him, to wait on his leading and to do what he shows me.

God desires our simple obedience to his voice, not our frantic activity

- Chapter Eight -

Love Never Fails

DRIVING up the road to the hospital was like travelling back in time. It was a dark, depressing old Victorian building spreading over several acres of ground and a sense of hopelessness and gloom hung over the whole place. To me it felt like a dungeon. My Mum had been a patient there for some years, and as she got older, I called out to God not to let her die in that place, a place that filled her with fear. I took hold of a promise in the Bible which says:

The cowering prisoners will soon be set free;
They will not die in their dungeon,
Nor will they lack bread.
Isaiah 51:14

Eventually she was moved to her own private room in a modern care home, so visiting her was much more pleasant and I felt that she finally had some privacy and dignity. When I'd visited the hospital she would ask just two questions, "Have you got any cigarettes?" and "Have you got any chocolate?" When she moved to the new care home, they helped her to stop smoking, so that left her with only one question to ask. She especially loved Cadbury's Milk Tray.

At the start of 2002 I had a strong sense that I should spend more time visiting, and in early March that year I got a call from the nurse at the care home saying Mum was unable to swallow and was being rushed to hospital. I hurried there to meet the ambulance and found that Mum was seriously ill. The next seven weeks would prove to be very difficult, but with an amazing surprise for me at the end.

The next seven weeks would prove to be very difficult, but with an amazing surprise for me at the end

During those weeks Sandie and her husband Les who were now living in Wales, and Andrew and his wife Catriona who now lived in England, travelled up a few times in order to visit at the hospital. Mum was not responding to any treatment, nor was she speaking to Andrew or Sandie. It pained my heart to watch them visit and make great efforts to communicate and be kind to her, only to receive no response. I remembered the pain of that Christmas Day years before, when Mum had told me she didn't know my name.

It was a horrible seven weeks, not only watching my Mum dying, but also seeing my brother and sister going through their pain. I wished, hoped and prayed that the love that I knew to be there deep down in my Mum's heart would come through all the fear and mental illness that affected her so badly, and that she would just say that she loved us. We all knew she was dying and that it was just a matter of time. I prayed hard those weeks, especially for Sandie and Andrew; I loved them and we loved each other. I prayed that God would somehow bring peace into this situation.

Steven and I were still leading the Prayer for the City ministry in Glasgow and we were holding a city-wide celebration with many churches coming together on the last Sunday of April. On the Thursday morning of that week we went to the large city centre church where we were to hold the event, in order to meet people and check everything was in place. This building wasn't too far from the hospital where Mum was, so afterwards I went on my own to sit at her bedside.

As I approached the ward I heard the same voice I had heard many times before. This time the Lord whispered into my heart saying to read Revelation 7:15-17. These verses say:

Therefore, they are before the throne of God
and serve him day and night in his temple;
and he who sits on the throne
will shelter them with his presence.
'Never again will they hunger;
never again will they thirst.
The sun will not beat down on them,'
nor any scorching heat.
For the Lamb at the centre of the throne
will be their shepherd;
he will lead them to springs of living water.
And God will wipe away every tear from their eyes.

As I sat by the bed I read those verses into myself a few times and then I said to Mum, "I want to read this to you. Is that OK?" I then read those words from the Bible to her and with tears in my eyes told her, "Jesus loves you and I love you." Amazingly, for the first time in those seven weeks my Mum smiled at me and said, "I know Jesus loves me. Helen, I have always known that, and I love you too and always have loved you." It took until the end of her life, but finally my mum told me of her love, a love I knew she did have, but was so unable to express. I hugged her and told her I had to go, Nicky was sitting her driving test and I needed to be home. (Nicky came in with the news that she'd passed).

It took until the end of her life, but finally my Mum told me of her love, a love I knew she did have, but was so unable to express

That was to be the last time I saw my Mum alive and wonderfully the last words I ever heard her speak were that she loved me and always had. I got a call from the hospital in the very early hours of Friday morning to say she had died. It was April 26th, my Gran's birthday. I cried in those early hours before it was light but I waited until a decent time before calling my sister and brother.

We had the city-wide celebration the following Sunday evening, where over a thousand people packed out the city centre building to praise and lift up the name of Jesus. Some people couldn't believe I was there just after my mum had died, but I wanted to be where Jesus my Healer was being worshipped by a large gathering of his people. I lifted up my head and eyes and it was as if I was looking straight into the face of my Heavenly Father. Steven was on one side of me and our dear friend Hugh Wallace was on the other. I was safe and in the best place.

Sandie and Andrew arrived back in Glasgow on the Monday, and Hugh, who was a local Church of Scotland minister, came to see us as I'd asked him to conduct the funeral. As we shared memories of our Mum I suddenly sobbed and sobbed. For about fifteen minutes I simply couldn't stop sobbing. The others just sat there quietly until I stopped. I had not cried like that at any of the other losses in my family, but here now, it was as if the floodgates of my emotions had been thrown open wide.

My Mum died on my Gran's birthday and the funeral was held on the 1st of May, the same day that I had met Steven twenty-one years earlier, a day that has such a special meaning to me. Somehow that was all part of my healing.

My Dad often told me that I was 'the apple of his eye', but until April 25th that year I can't remember my Mum ever saying that she loved me. I'd often judged my parents, for the way they had brought us up, my Mum in her illness and my Dad in his drinking. I had often thought, "Why couldn't they just be normal parents?" I had been told by others that if my dad hadn't married my mum then he wouldn't have become an alcoholic – it was all her fault. When I'd become depressed I'd imagined that everything was my fault, that Steven would be better off without me and that I would ruin his life. I had judged and blamed my Mum, not consciously, but deep in my soul. We reap what we sow until Jesus steps into our lives to redeem. The judgement and blame that I had passed came back on me as I judged myself and blamed myself during that dark period of my life.

God's healing has sometimes come to me in immediate ways and at other times through much longer processes. What I now know is this: he has freed me from the vicious circle of judgement and taken away my pain and shame. I believe God's healing work over the years freed me and positioned me finally to interact meaningfully with my mother, even on her deathbed; to hear her speak the name of Jesus and tell me of her love. I also discovered the faithfulness of God's word that "the prisoners will not die in their dungeons." We have seen and will continue to see prisoners of darkness and depression set free.

We reap what we sow until Jesus steps into our lives to redeem

We have seen and will continue to see prisoners of darkness and depression set free

A number of years ago, when we were ministering to a woman who had severe depression, I had a powerful dream. In the dream she and I were in what appeared to be a prisoner of war camp. We, along with other people, were prisoners there, though we were the significant ones in the dream. We were deep down in the depths of a dungeon that had large walls with barbed wire on top. Suddenly a shaft of light appeared and a thick, knotted rope was thrown down to me. Using the knots as steps for my feet, I climbed the rope to the top where the light was coming from and I was free.

The commander of the camp was strutting about in a very proud manner announcing that no-one ever escapes from this place. I went to run off but then realised that I had left my friend behind and that I must go back to get her out. I went back and threw the rope down to her calling out, "Grab hold, you can be free too." At first she wouldn't take it, but I repeated over and over, "I am free, you can be too." Then she grabbed hold of the rope and I pulled her up to freedom.

After this we went to the commander of the camp and I said to him, "You strut around and pride yourself that no-one can escape from your hold. But we are free and you can't hold us any longer and others can be free too."

The woman in my dream who we were helping was completely freed from that depression very soon after. It was in our living room as Steven and another friend prayed for her in Jesus' name. The power of God fell on her and she shook for about half an hour. After that she was totally well. She had been like me, depressed and heading for hospital, but God broke in and freed her.

God has changed my life and we have seen him change many others too. Let's lift up our eyes and see what God is doing and open our ears to hear what he says.

God has changed my life and we have seen him change many others too

At the beginning of John's gospel, Jesus is called 'The Word'. We read,

The Word became flesh and made his dwelling among us. We have seen his glory, the glory of the one and only Son, who came from the Father, full of grace and truth.

John 1:14

His grace brings forgiveness to us, enabling us to forgive others and ourselves. It allows healing to flow even to the deepest wounds. By his grace we can hear the truth and live in the truth. Knowing the truth, as Jesus said, sets us free (John 8:32). We don't need to hide from the truth, no matter how painful it is. Jesus offers grace, healing and freedom to each one of us.

- Chapter Nine -

No More Dungeons

I stepped over a stile into the most lush, green pastures I had ever seen. There, in this vision, I saw a shepherd with his staff in his hand. I drew alongside him and walked by his side through those beautiful fields until we came to a barn. He was beckoning me to open the barn door but I seemed to be afraid. I knew the barn was full - was I ready to accept the abundance that was there? I did eventually open the door and as it opened the grain spilled out, pouring right over the top of me. God has an abundance of all things in store for us.

'Enough' was the word that God spoke on the day that changed my life. Since then I have discovered God's 'enough' in many ways. The 23rd Psalm portrays God as our Shepherd, a relationship that means we need lack nothing. He leads us and makes us lie down in luscious green pastures; he lavishes his grace and love upon us.

God restores us, at the expense of Jesus' death on the cross, so that we can each play our part in the purposes of his Kingdom

To me one of the most powerful phrases of the Bible is found in the next line of this famous Psalm where David says, "He restores my soul." God has been, and still is, restoring my soul, making me more and more into the person he always intended me to be. If an old, dilapidated building is restored at great expense, it would be a waste for it to sit empty and not be used for any purpose. God restores us, at the expense of Jesus' death on the cross, so that we can each play our part in the purposes of his Kingdom.

God wants to heal us from past wounds, redeem our failings, and free us from the bonds of judgements we have passed on ourselves and other people. He heals and liberates us, so that he can then bring us into the fullness of the life of adventure that Jesus modelled for us.

I thank God every day that he has changed my life and lifted me up in his love and power, enabling me to partner with the Holy Spirit in doing the works of his Kingdom on earth today. When I think back to the insecure and fearful little child I once was, I am amazed at God's work of grace that has equipped me to stand strong in his love; to preach and teach in many places, to heal the sick and set free those whose lives are tormented and bound in chains.

I used to live with my eyes down, looking at my toes and avoiding the gaze of other people, feeling insignificant like a little worm. But God's word has spoken powerfully into my life:

"So do not fear, for I am with you; do not be dismayed, for I am your God.
I will strengthen you and help you; I will uphold you with my righteous right hand."
Isaiah 41:10

This has given me courage and true boldness, filling me with joy, peace and hope, making me into a secure woman who will now look anyone in the eye without fear.

God had opened my eyes; I was seeing myself, my parents, my surroundings and even the grass differently. One time, as God's healing was becoming more apparent in my life, we were visiting Millport on the island of Great Cumbrae, a famous day trip venue for people from Glasgow. There, on the island, was a stretch of grass that suddenly looked so green. I exclaimed out loud, almost yelling, about how beautifully green this grass was to me. Steven and the friends with us looked at me and said, "Yeah, it is green, Helen, grass is always green." However, something had been awakened in me and I was beginning to see everything in a new light.

God has a purpose for each of us, but I think a lot of people can miss it. Our greatest need is truly to know God – the loving Heavenly Father – and to find his purpose for our lives. The outworking of that purpose might be quite different for each one of us, but it is always good. As we believe in Jesus, and let him free us from whatever might hold us back, we can step into all that he wants to open up before us.

God has a purpose for each of us, but I think a lot of people can miss it

That night at 2am when God's authoritative word "Enough" came into my ears and my heart, I knew I was changed forever and he had taken hold of me. It was a word that boomed into the darkness, banishing it from my life. It was a word that laid claim to me – his treasured possession –

and no other power would ever have a claim on me again. Now my aim is to do what the Apostle Paul said:

I press on to take hold of that for which Christ Jesus took hold of me.
Philippians 3:12

God wants to fill you with hope for today and for the future, no matter what the past has looked like. He wants to transform you into a radiant person who shines with his love, joy and peace. Let him speak his words of life over you – words of healing, words of deliverance, words of hope, words of purpose and calling, and words of affirmation and permission.

It was a word that laid claim to me – his treasured possession – and no other power would ever have a claim on me again

When Jesus was baptised, the heavens were opened and the Holy Spirit descended, resting and remaining upon him. Then a voice spoke: that wonderful voice of the Father,

"You are my Son, whom I love; with you I am well pleased."
Luke 3:22

These words would sustain Jesus through every temptation, every trial and all his suffering. They would propel him forward in his amazing life and work. The Father now speaks those words to us who are in Christ. These are words that give us identity as his sons and daughters. This is where we find our true identity, not in our occupation - which will one day end, not in how we've perceived ourselves, not based on how others have treated us, nor from anything else good or bad. The eternal identity that God wants to bestow on each of us is to be his child.

The eternal identity that God wants to bestow on each of us is to be his child

I see myself in a whole new light now – the light of Jesus. I used to see myself so very differently. So much so that I didn't ever want to look in a mirror; I detested mirrors. My sister in law was visiting us one weekend, and when she was drying her hair in the morning, she asked me, "Where will I find a mirror?" "You won't" I replied, "I hate mirrors." Now I find myself about to hang the biggest mirror I can in our living room! A mirror shows clearly what is there and I am no longer ashamed or afraid of what I see reflected.

Those words from the Father assure us of his love and of his pleasure in us. As we give our lives to Jesus Christ and truly identify with him, we can know the Father's eternal, undying love which never fails and never changes. Not only that, but we can also know his pleasure, and hear him say that he is pleased with us. Maybe not everything we think, say and do always pleases him, but as his children, simply who we are brings him pleasure.

Living in this identity, secure in his love, armed with his affirmation and anointed by the Holy Spirit, we can do the very things Jesus did; we can live a life that shapes history. No matter how grand or how lowly our beginnings, no matter how well thought of or insignificant we've seemed; we can all rise up through Jesus Christ to do great exploits.

Today is the beginning of the rest of your life. Why remain held back by your past, trapped in judgements and unforgiveness? Why let your life be ruled by the expectations that others have placed on you? Why be hemmed in by the restricted view you've had of yourself? Will you merely meander through life in the familiar patterns of your existence? Have you had 'enough' of the past? Step out into the destiny that God has for you in Christ Jesus.

We can all rise up through Jesus Christ to do great exploits

The world waits for people like you and me to enter into our God-given purpose. Let us rise up like the eagle and soar into the vast expanse of God's great plan.

Prayers of Healing and Blessing

A Blessing:

May God the Father, the One from whom every family derives its name, bless you, strengthen you and protect you.

May you know the affirmation of his love and the delight that he takes in you as his child.

Know that he formed you in your mother's womb and that your birth was in his eternal plan.

Today I say to you that you are loved, wanted and that you belong in God's family. You have a special purpose, to do the works God planned for you before you were born. You have permission to do great things.

I call forth the potential within you. I call you to rise up in Jesus Christ to be and to do all that he has purposed for you. May the life that is in you be fully nurtured and come to blossom and to full fruitfulness. May you make a difference for good in this world.

May the peace of Christ guard your heart and mind, now and always.

A Prayer to Honour Your Parents:

I choose today to honour my mother and my father. I accept them as my parents, the ones through who I came to be. I forgive any wrongs that they did to me, and I forgive any perceived failings that I saw in them.

I thank God for my parents and for all the good I have received from them.

I turn from and renounce any judgements that I have passed concerning my mother or my father. I break the power of that process of judgement today in Jesus name.

As I continue to choose to honour my mother and my father (and their memory), I claim the promise of God's word that life will go well for me and I will enjoy long life (Ephesians 6:2-3).

A Prayer for Healing:

Father, I ask for healing in my body, mind and emotions (specify any particular condition).

I ask forgiveness for my wrong doing and I choose to forgive those who have wronged me in any way (take a few minutes and consider who and what is involved here).

I believe that you are able and willing to heal me right now.

I ask you to send your word into my body and mind, and to stretch out your hand of healing upon me.

I receive your healing by faith in the name of Jesus Christ.

A Prayer for Salvation:

I recognise today that I am separated from God and that I need to be, and can be reconciled to God through Jesus Christ who died on the cross for my wrong doing.

I ask you, Father God, to forgive all my wrongs – in actions, words, thoughts, and failings to act in right ways.

I choose to turn my life to you and receive your gift of new life in Jesus Christ.

I believe that Jesus died for me on the cross and that he is risen from the dead. I ask that you, Jesus, would come and make your home in me today.

I ask you to impart your Holy Spirit to me now. Thank you for giving me new life.

(If you have prayed this prayer for the first time in your life do make every effort to connect with a group of Christians where you can learn about your new life and faith. If you need help with this then contact us).

Other Publications

Available from

www.healingrooms-scotland.com

RELEASING HEALING

Steven Anderson

£6.99

Releasing Healing by Steven Anderson sets forth a vision of what is possible for a church that truly believes. The book tackles many of the questions that surround the ministry of healing and encourages us to press forward, growing in understanding, developing a more effective healing ministry and taking the healing power of Christ into our communities and to the nations.

KNOCK! KNOCK!

Kirsten Coulter

£6.99

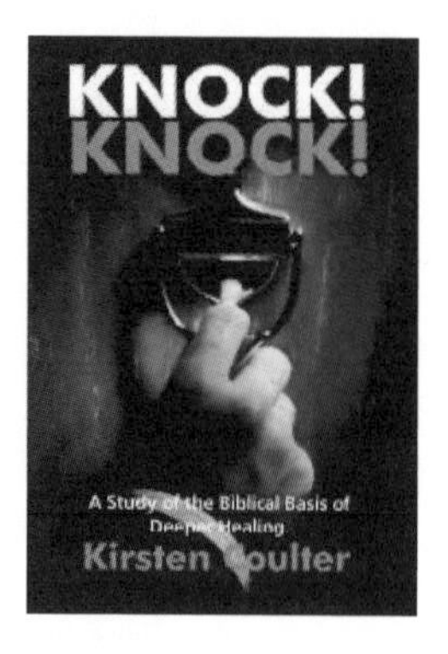

This book takes a fresh look at many well-known Bible stories, seeing them from the perspective of a generous, compassionate God, who wants us to be at peace with ourselves, with each other, and above all with himself.

WHEN GOD SPEAKS CD

Allan McKinlay

£10

Allan McKinlay's Album **When God Speaks** is available through Healing Rooms Scotland or via his website www.allanmckinlay.com. Allan is a Scottish worship leader and singer/songwriter. This newly released album features popular songs such as Only One, Dry Bones, He Reigns and When God Speaks.

Helen Anderson
The Day That Changed My Life

TO CONTACT THE AUTHOR

Write to:

Healing Rooms Scotland
PO Box 7010
Glasgow
G76 7UL
U.K.

E-mail:

admin@healingrooms-scotland.com

Telephone:

0141 637 4445